BRITISH RAILWAYS

PAST and PRESENT

No 48

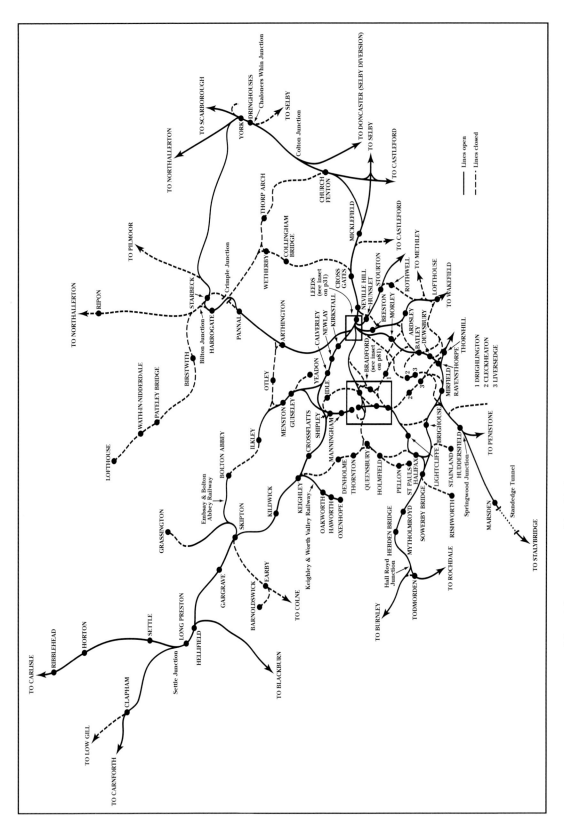

Map of the area covered by this book, showing locations featured or referred to in the text.

BRITISH RAILWAYS

PAST and PRESENT

No 48

Yorkshire: The West Riding
Part 1: Lines around York, Leeds, Bradford, Huddersfield, Halifax, Harrogate and Skipton

Paul Shannon and John Hillmer

Past and
Present

Past & Present Publishing Ltd

© Paul Shannon & John Hillmer 2005

First published in 2005
Reprinted 2008

British Library Cataloguing in Publication Data

A catalogue record for this book is available from the British Library.

ISBN 978 1 85895 240 6

Past & Present Publishing Ltd
The Trundle
Ringstead Road
Great Addington
Kettering
Northants NN14 4BW

Tel/Fax: 01536 330588
email: sales@nostalgiacollection.com
Website: www.nostalgiacollection.com

Printed and bound in the Czech Republic

WORTLEY JUNCTION: Ex-LMS '4F' 0-6-0 No 44186 passes Wortley Junction, on the MR/NER approach to Leeds, with a rake of empty high-sided coal and coke wagons on 9 March 1961.

Electrification gave a new lease of life to the Airedale and Wharfedale lines in the 1990s. The track layout at Wortley Junction has been greatly simplified, but the four tracks that remain carry a frequent passenger service as well as freight to and from the Settle & Carlisle line. EMU No 333008 forms the 1418 service from Skipton to Leeds on 19 February 2004. *Gavin Morrison/PDS*

CONTENTS

BIBLIOGRAPHY

ABC British Railways Locomotives, combined volumes: various years (Ian Allan)
Allen, D., and Woolstenholmes, C. J. *A Pictorial Survey of Railway Signalling* (OPC)
Baker, S. J. *Rail Atlas of Great Britain and Ireland*, various editions (OPC)
Bolger, Paul *BR Steam Motive Power Depots: LMR* (Ian Allan)
Butt, R. V. J. *The Directory of Railway Stations* (Patrick Stephens)
Chapman, Stephen, and Rose, Peter *Railway Memories No 6 Ardsley, Wakefield and Normanton* (Bellcode)
Coates, Noel *150 Years of the Lancashire & Yorkshire Railway* (Hawkshill Publishing)
Earnshaw, Alan *Pennine Branch Lines* (Ian Allan)
   The Lancashire & Yorkshire Railway (Ian Allan)
Joy, David *A Regional History of the Railways of Great Britain: Volume 8 South and West Yorkshire* (David & Charles)
Old Ordnance Survey Maps: various (Alan Godfrey Maps)
Rhodes, Michael, and Shannon, Paul *Freight Only Yearbook, Nos 1 and 2* (Silver Link Publishing)
Shannon, Paul *ABC Railway Freight Operations* (Ian Allan)
Whitaker, Alan, and Myland, Brian *Railway Memories No 4 Bradford* (Bellcode)
Wignall, C. J. *Complete British Railways Maps and Gazetteer 1830-1981* (OPC)

Back issues of:
Branch Line News
Modern Railways
Rail
Railway Magazine
The Railway Observer
Railway World

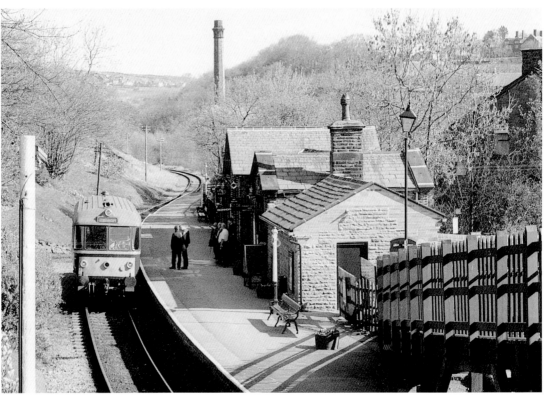

INTRODUCTION

From the industrial towns of the Calder and Aire valleys to the rural outposts of the Yorkshire Dales, the area covered in this book offers huge variety of scenery and railway history.

The rich traffic potential of the woollen towns such as Bradford, Leeds and Halifax attracted a large number of competing railway companies. By the early years of the 20th century the Lancashire & Yorkshire Railway (L&YR), Great Northern Railway (GNR), North Eastern Railway (NER), Midland Railway (MR) and London & North Western Railway (LNWR) were all established in the area, sometimes operating in isolation from each other – as at Bradford, where railway rivalry left the town with the handicap of two unconnected termini – and sometimes entering into complex inter-company agreements – as at Leeds, where both the pre-Grouping stations were joint facilities.

The rural landscape north of the Aire valley did not support competing railway routes. The Midland Railway held the monopoly of lines to the north and west of Keighley, while the NER was virtually the sole operator in the area north-east of Leeds. A curious exception was the Nidd Valley Light Railway, an independent line built by Bradford Corporation to convey materials and men for the building of two reservoirs.

After the 1923 Grouping, both the London, Midland & Scottish Railway (LMS) and London & North Eastern Railway (LNER) operated substantial networks in the West Riding. The three trans-Pennine routes via Standedge, Hebden Bridge and Skipton all belonged to the LMS, while the LNER was dominant on the eastern side of the area. But the LMS reached as far east as Goole over former L&YR metals, while the LNER stretched to Keighley in the west via the ex-GNR branch from Queensbury. There was still a great deal of duplication – and a great deal of variety in terms of railway infrastructure and motive power.

The few minor line closures before the Second World War paled into insignificance when British Railways started withdrawing unremunerative services in the 1950s. Among the first lines to go were the Rishworth and Stainland branches south of Halifax and the ex-GNR 'Alpine' railway linking Halifax, Keighley and Bradford. Several links around Dewsbury and Batley were also axed, as was the former East & West Yorkshire Union Railway (E&WYU) line via Robin Hood. But rural lines in the north remained largely intact, other than the Nidd Valley Railway, which had closed in 1930.

The Beeching Report of 1962 sealed the fate of many more routes, including the former main line north of Harrogate and most of the remaining rural branches. Also targeted for closure were many local services in the area bounded by Leeds, Bradford, Halifax and Dewsbury. However, not all the Beeching closure plans were approved: the lines from Harrogate to York and from Leeds/Bradford to Ilkley were reprieved and are still in operation today.

The 'modern image' reached the West Riding as early as the mid-1950s when the first diesel multiple units (DMUs) entered service, but the transition from steam to diesel traction was not complete until 1968. There was still much variety on the steam front up to the mid-1960s, with former LNER and LMS types as well as BR Standard designs.

HAWORTH: It is still possible to step into the past on the Worth Valley line thanks to the pioneering efforts of the Keighley & Worth Valley Railway preservation society in the 1960s. Our 'past' photograph records Haworth station on 3 June 1960, two years before the branch was abandoned by British Railways. Ivatt 2-6-2T No 41326 is hauling a push-pull train from Keighley to Oxenhope.

Today's scene of 13 April 2004 could almost have been taken in the 1960s, as German-built railbus No 79964 pauses with the 0955 Keighley-Oxenhope service. The closed-circuit television camera on the left is a sadly necessary concession to modern times. *Gavin Morrison/JCH*

The re-opening of Baildon station in 1973 signalled the beginning of a new era for local passenger services around Leeds and Bradford. There was good support from the local Passenger Transport Executive, and the spread of Paytrain operation was an incentive to open additional stations without the costs of providing resident staff. Between 1982 and 1992 BR provided more than a dozen new or re-opened stations in the area covered by this book, as well as resuming all-year-round local services on the reprieved Settle & Carlisle line. Things have moved more slowly since privatisation, but the direct service between Huddersfield and Halifax via Brighouse finally restarted in 2000.

Electric services reached Leeds in 1988 as part of the East Coast Main Line modernisation programme. A more surprising development was the extension of overhead wires to Bradford, Skipton and Ilkley, complete with comfortable new trains and a greatly enhanced service frequency. Elsewhere in the region, almost all trains are worked by second-generation diesel units, though Arriva Trains Northern heralded a temporary return to locomotive haulage when it hired a pair of Class 37s for a Knaresborough-Leeds-Carlisle diagram in 2004.

Several scenes in this book depict the rapidly changing freight scene, with many terminal and siding closures reflecting the shift towards a smaller number of regular high-volume flows. Just seven freight terminals remain in use at the time of writing in the area covered by this book: Rylstone (Tilcon quarry), Shipley (scrapyard), Laisterdyke (scrapyard), Hunslet (Tilcon stone terminal and opencast coal loading) and Stourton (Freightliner and RMC stone terminal). Although trans-Pennine freight has declined, the Settle & Carlisle line is busy with trainloads of coal and gypsum, and the East Coast route through York still carries a wide range of freight.

One of the earliest preservation schemes in Britain was the re-opening of the Worth Valley branch in 1968, just six years after its closure by the British Transport Commission. More than three decades later, the branch is still a popular tourist attraction. The Embsay Steam Railway was established in 1981 on part of the former through route between Skipton and Ilkley. A third preservation site in the area is the Middleton Railway, on the site of the waggonway opened in 1758.

Inevitably, most pairs of photographs in this book show a reduction in railway facilities, although there are some notable exceptions such as Stourton Freightliner terminal and Crossflatts station. Many lineside views are now obscured by undergrowth or disfigured by Network Rail's metallic palisade fencing. Some closed lines have disappeared without trace, which meant that the authors had to rely on comparing old and new large-scale Ordnance Survey maps.

We wish to thank all those who contributed 'past' photographs, particularly Gavin Morrison, without whom much of the book would not have been possible. We are also grateful to Richard Casserley, Bryan Wilson, Peter Rose and Paul Fletcher for checking caption material, to Geraldine Hillmer for digital prints, and to Kirklees Community History Service for permission to use the picture of Huddersfield station façade.

John Hillmer, Wilmslow
Paul Shannon, Chester

York

YORK: 'K1' 2-6-0 No 62028 waits for a signal before proceeding to the south end of the station on 26 May 1966. The building on the right, behind the signal gantry, had been one of the station signal boxes until 1951.

The buildings on the main up platform remained much as they were when photographed on 18 February 2004, with a Virgin-operated 'Voyager' Class 220 diesel unit on a Cross Country service standing at the principal down platform. The biggest change has been the removal of the centre through roads, while the overhead wires for 25kV electrification are barely conspicuous. *Roger Siviter/JCH*

YORK: In 1976 Class 40 No 40154 enters the station from the north with a mixed train of parcels vans, likely to be the Heaton to Manchester Red Bank newspaper empties; the first three carriages are LMS, GWR and BR Standard types respectively. The crossover in the foreground gave access from the main down platform to the Scarborough line.

The track remodelling completed in 1988 included the removal of the centre roads and the Scarborough line crossover. A relative newcomer to the East Coast Main Line is this Virgin 220 'Voyager' unit, leaving for Newcastle as the 0610 service from Southampton on 18 February 2004. *Both JCH*

YORK: This early-20th-century postcard shows the curve through the station, looking north. A number of station staff on both platforms await the arrival of the next trains. There is a notice on the up platform stating 'To the GN C.C.C.E. & Midland Companies offices'.

Today's view, taken on 18 February 2004, shows remarkably little change, other than the trappings of electrification and the disappearance of the centre through roads. The footbridge and clock remain. *John Ryan collection/JCH*

YORK: At the south end of York station, ex-LNER 'A3' 4-6-2 No 60083 *Sir Hugo* is about to pilot ex-LMS 'Black Five' 4-6-0 No 45336 on the Newcastle to Manchester empty van train on 12 April 1959. This train was routinely double-headed south of York.

Arriva trans-Pennine Class 158 No 158809 leaves with the 1117 Newcastle-Manchester Airport service on 18 February 2004. Apart from the electrification wires and supports and some track rationalisation, the scene has not changed much in the 45 years between the two photographs. Even the former York & North Midland Railway locomotive erecting shops still stand to the right of the car park. *David Holmes/JCH*

YORK: Dated 1 May 1966, this interior shot of York North shed illustrates so vividly the atmosphere of a roundhouse. From left to right are a BR Standard 4MT 2-6-0, a 'B1' 4-6-0 and ex-LNER 'V2' 2-6-2 No 60824 with a 64A shedplate (St Margaret's, Edinburgh).

The shed closed to steam in 1967 and completely in 1973. It then became the home of the National Railway Museum in 1975. A £2 million National Lottery grant in 1998 enabled the museum to extend into the roundhouse, and exhibited on the turntable on 18 February 2004 is GNR Stirling 'Single' 4-2-2 No 1, built in 1870. This engine may well have reached as far north as York during its working life. *Roger Siviter/JCH*

YORK HOLGATE: This fine view looking north from Holgate bridge in the pre-Grouping era shows Midland Railway '2P' 4-4-0 No 402 leaving York with a southbound express. Partly obscured by the smoke on the right is Queen Street engine shed, which was converted from the works boiler shop of the York & North Midland Railway in 1909 and was to remain in use with the LMS until 1932.

Several generations of traction have come and gone in the 70-plus years between the two photographs. Major resignalling schemes took place in 1951 and 1989, the latter in conjunction with electrification. On 18 February 2004 an InterCity 225 unit restarts from York with the 1000 Glasgow Central to London King's Cross service. *John Ryan collection/PDS*

DRINGHOUSES yard was remodelled in 1961 to bring it in line with the norms of the 1955 Modernisation Plan. Although small in comparison with the likes of Healey Mills and Doncaster, Dringhouses handled a significant amount of through traffic as well as wagonloads to and from York itself. It survived into the Speedlink era mainly thanks to the confectionery business from Rowntree-Mackintosh. On 6 August 1986 Class 47 No 47305 pulls out of the yard with 6O44, the 1605 Tyneside Central Freight Depot to Paddock Wood Speedlink working.

The loss of the Rowntree-Mackintosh traffic in 1987 sealed the fate of Dringhouses yard, and a housing estate now occupies the site. 'Voyager' unit No 220028 speeds past with the 1035 service from Edinburgh to Exeter St David's on 18 February 2004. *Both PDS*

CHALONERS WHIN JUNCTION: Class 'K1' 2-6-0 No 62066 takes the Selby line at Chaloners Whin Junction with an up mixed goods train in June 1961. The East Coast Main Line curved sharply at this point because the first railway to reach York from the south was the line from Normanton, completed in 1840, the line from Selby being added in 1871.

The foreground in today's photograph is almost a return to pre-1871 days: the cutting that once carried the East Coast Main Line has been filled in and the site is returning to nature. BR closed the section between Selby and Chaloners Whin Junction in 1983 when the prospect of mining subsidence forced the construction of the 14-mile 'Selby Diversion' between Temple Hirst Junction and Colton Junction – Britain's first new double-track main line since the opening of the GCR's London extension at the end of the 19th century. A Class 158 unit can just be seen approaching York on the line from Colton Junction on 18 February 2004. *Noel Machell/PDS*

CHURCH FENTON was a double junction on the York & North Midland Railway approach to York, with the line from Leeds via Micklefield converging from the south and the branch to Wetherby and Harrogate diverging to the north. The spacious five-platform station, completed in 1904 to replace an earlier facility, is pictured facing north on 21 April 1954. The building on the far left is the original station house, dating back to 1847.

Today Church Fenton is still a junction, with routes from Leeds and Castleford converging behind the photographer. The 1847 station house survives as a well-maintained private dwelling. The station retains four through platforms – which seems generous for today's sparse train service – but it became an unstaffed halt in 1989 and the platform buildings were demolished soon afterwards. Unit No 158766 calls for modest custom as the 1514 York to Manchester Victoria service on 24 January 2004. *H. C. Casserley/PDS*

Around Harrogate

THORP ARCH station, between Church Fenton and Wetherby, was opened by the York & North Midland Railway in 1847. The fine Tudor-Gothic buildings on the westbound platform are pictured from a passing train on 21 April 1954. A curious feature was the small stone shelter over the entrance to the booking office.

BR closed Thorp Arch station in 1964. Forty years later the building survives as a private house, having kept its original features with remarkably little alteration. The close-up view of 24 January 2004 shows scaffolding in place for essential maintenance – the ownership of a 19th-century listed building does not come cheap! *H. C. Casserley/PDS*

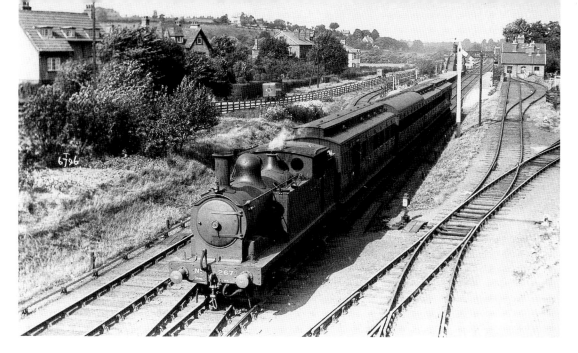

COLLINGHAM BRIDGE was the last station before Wetherby on the line from Leeds. Ex-NER Class 'N8' 0-6-2T No 267 has just made its call with a local train to Leeds in the summer of 1933. Some vintage commercial road transport completes the period scene.

The Leeds-Wetherby line survived into the BR era; even Liverpool to Newcastle expresses were routed this way until the early 1960s in order to avoid a reversal at Leeds City. However, the Beeching Report targeted all three lines radiating from Wetherby and BR closed the Leeds-Wetherby-Harrogate route completely in 1964. By 24 January 2004 part of the former railway cutting had been filled to create a new road junction, but two houses on the left provide a clear link with the 'past' picture. *R. M. Casserley collection/PDS*

HARROGATE: The unusual layout of the railways around Harrogate made it possible for Leeds trains to depart in either direction – north via Starbeck or south via Crimple. Class 'D49' 4-4-0 No 62740 *The Bedale* simmers with the 5.30pm departure to Leeds via Starbeck and Horsforth on 5 August 1957.

Harrogate station lost its NER awnings in the 1950s and the track layout has seen some rationalisation, although one centre road remains in use for stabling diesel units overnight. An interesting working in 2004 was this rake of air-conditioned Mark II coaches 'top-and-tailed' by EWS Class 37s, covering a peak-hour service between Knaresborough and Leeds and a daytime return trip between Leeds and Carlisle. Nos 37405 and 37411 *The Scottish Railway Preservation Society* provide the power for the 0758 departure from Knaresborough on 25 March. *David Holmes/PDS*

21

HARROGATE: The present station at Harrogate dates back to 1862, when the NER opened new connections between Pannal Junction and Crimple Junction and between Harrogate and Bilton Junction to enable its Leeds to Thirsk trains to serve the town; previously they had called at Starbeck, nearly 2 miles from central Harrogate. Class 'V2' 2-6-2 No 60929 enters the north end of Harrogate station with the 11.15 Saturdays-only Newcastle to Llandudno train on 28 June 1958.

The sidings and bay on the east side of the station have been removed, but trains departing for Knaresborough and York are still controlled by the same bracket semaphore signal – now looking rather the worse for wear – as in 1958. Unit No 144021 forms the 0742 departure to York on 25 March 2004. *David Holmes/PDS*

HARROGATE: Coal drops were a feature of many goods yards on former NER metals, enabling easy discharge from hopper wagons. Two HTV/HTO wagons are visible on Harrogate 'drops' as a Metropolitan-Cammell two-car unit, Nos E50134 and E56063, departs with a local service to York on 6 September 1980.

The goods depot remained open for coal traffic until 1984, but since then the sidings have given way to commercial development. The wooden-posted signal has been replaced by a tubular steel type, and the boundary wall on the right is now topped by a spiked metal fence. Unit No 156454 forms the 0742 service from Harrogate to York on 26 March 2004. *Both PDS*

RIPON: The former Leeds & Thirsk Railway main line through Ripon continued to carry long-distance traffic until its closure in March 1967. English Electric Type 4 (later Class 40) No D278 crosses the River Ure on the approach to Ripon with a Liverpool to Newcastle express on 3 December 1966. Three typical cars of the era are parked outside the garage on the left – an Austin A40, a Ford Popular and a Morris Minor van.

The absence of a railway viaduct over the Ure today is one of the main stumbling blocks to the proposed rebuilding of the Harrogate to Ripon railway. Only the road junction confirms the location for the 'present' photograph of 24 January 2004. *Gavin Morrison/PDS*

RIPON: The Leeds Northern Railway provided new station buildings for Ripon in 1855, replacing the original facilities built by the Leeds & Thirsk. The platform awnings were clad with slates on boards, which must have made them rather dark for waiting passengers. The station is pictured facing north on 26 June 1950.

Passenger services were withdrawn in 1967 and goods traffic ceased two years later. The station buildings lay derelict for many years, but have recently been sympathetically incorporated into a housing development, as pictured on 24 January 2004. It would now be necessary to find a new station site if ever the line from Harrogate were re-opened. *H. C. Casserley/PDS*

BIRSTWITH: The NER Pateley Bridge branch closed to passengers in 1951 but remained open for goods traffic for another 13 years. The 'Nidd Valley Railtour', organised by the Railway Correspondence & Travel Society, brings a brief revival to Birstwith station on 19 October 1963 as it pauses for a photo stop. The locomotive is Class 4 2-6-4T No 42409.

The trackbed was sold off piecemeal after closure and a housing estate was built on the former goods yard at Birstwith. This was the scene on 24 January 2004. *R. M. Casserley/PDS*

PATELEY BRIDGE: The disused but intact ex-NER station at Pateley Bridge is pictured on 19 October 1963, while railtour passengers enjoy a few minutes of exploration. The station house with its stepped gables was similar to others on the line, but the conservatory-type shelter on the platform was unusual. Behind the photographer, the track had originally continued over a level crossing to form an end-on junction with the Nidd Valley Railway.

The station house has survived almost intact for more than half a century after the line closed to passengers. However, there is no trace of the former railway in the 'present' photograph of 24 January 2004; the stone wall in front of the house gives the misleading impression that the road has always been there. *R. M. Casserley/PDS*

PATELEY BRIDGE: The Nidd Valley Light Railway was built by Bradford Corporation to carry workmen and materials for the construction of Scar House and Angram reservoirs. It started out as a narrow-gauge line but was converted to standard gauge in 1906/07, enabling goods traffic to be worked through from the NER. Passenger services operated between Pateley Bridge and Lofthouse, first using steam locomotives and four-wheeled coaches until a steam railcar was acquired from the GWR. This mid-1920s scene shows 0-6-0ST *Blythe* waiting to depart from the NVLR terminus at Pateley Bridge.

More than 60 years after closure, the NVLR station building is still standing, surrounded by a highways maintenance yard. The 'present' photograph is dated 24 January 2004. *R. M. Casserley collection/PDS*

WATH-IN-NIDDERDALE: Hopes that the NVLR might remain an economic proposition after the reservoirs were completed proved to be unrealistic and the passenger service was withdrawn in December 1929. The railway closed completely in 1936 and the track was lifted almost immediately. The neat platform and station house at Wath-in-Nidderdale are pictured in 1928; the house was already in private occupation by this time.

Although much of the track bed can still be traced, there is nothing to suggest that Rhyllstone House once had a railway running past its front door. The much extended former station house is pictured on 24 January 2004. *R. M. Casserley collection/PDS*

Around Leeds

NEVILLE HILL: 'Britannia' 4-6-2 No 70015 *Apollo* pilots 'Black Five' 4-6-0 No 45200 out of Neville Hill yard on the last steam-worked 'Red Bank vans' – newspaper empties returning to Red Bank carriage sidings near Manchester Victoria – on 3 July 1966. The tracks curving round to the right are the NER branch to Hunslet Goods.

   The line between Leeds station and Neville Hill was electrified as part of the East Coast scheme so that electric trains could be serviced and stabled at Neville Hill depot. An InterCity 225 rake can be seen in the background as Class 60 No 60056 *William Beveridge* pulls away with 6M54, the 1056 Hunslet to Stanlow empty tank train, on 18 February 1995. This scene too has now passed into history: the oil traffic from Stanlow ceased in 1998 and the last oil train to Hunslet ran in 2002. *Gavin Morrison/PDS*

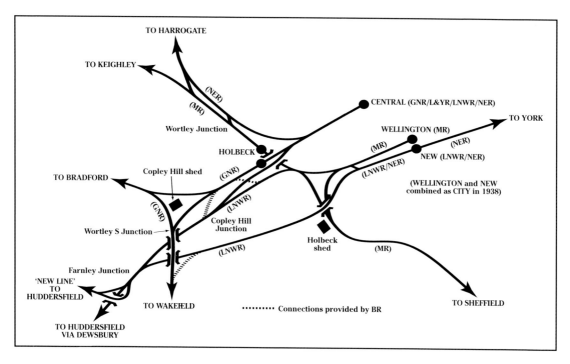

The railways of Leeds.

CROSS GATES: Just over 4 miles east of Leeds, the station was opened by the Leeds & Selby Railway in September 1834, closed in 1840, but re-opened after 10 years by the York & North Midland Railway. On 13 April 1964 preserved ex-LNER 2-6-0 No 3442 *The Great Marquess* takes a three-coach special eastwards.

Little has changed in the 40 years between the photos, although the iron footbridge is no longer in use. The semaphore signals have gone but the Station Hotel remains. No 3442 is still in preservation, based on the Severn Valley Railway at the time of writing, while in the 'present' picture of 2 March 2004 a three-car Class 158 unit heads east. *Gavin Morrison/JCH*

HUNSLET: Peppercorn 'A1' 4-6-2 No 60123 *H. A. Ivatt* heads the 'Harrogate Sunday Pullman' through Hunslet, on the former Midland Railway approach to Leeds, on 18 September 1960. This was a diversion due to engineering work on the direct ex-GNR line through Wakefield.

A rather humbler train provides the focal point for the 'present' photograph, taken on 19 February 2004, as 'Pacer' No 142066 forms the 1208 all-stations service from Sheffield to Leeds. The trackwork has been simplified, but even more striking is the loss of all the lineside industrial buildings visible in 1960. *David Holmes/PDS*

HUNSLET: The narrow platforms of Hunslet station are pictured on 7 May 1960, as Stanier Class 3MT 2-6-2T No 40148 calls with the 6.20pm Leeds City to Cudworth local train. The closure of Hunslet station was just five weeks away, while No 40148 was to survive until 1962.

No trace of the station remains today, as unit No 142066 ambles along as the 1134 Leeds to Sheffield service. The back-to-back terraces in the earlier photograph have given way to light industrial development, but there is also still a lot of derelict land in this part of Leeds. The rusty siding on the right gave access to Hunslet locomotive works. *David Holmes/PDS*

HUNSLET: The down sidings at Hunslet became a gathering point for wagonload traffic in the Speedlink era, while Balm Road goods depot on the up side of the line specialised in limestone traffic from Peak Forest. Class 31 No 31175 departs with 8K58, the 1415 Hunslet to Healey Mills Speedlink trip working, on 15 August 1986. The load includes seven POA wagons with scrap that had probably come from Shipley.

Hunslet yard was abandoned after the closure of Speedlink, while the limestone traffic to Balm Road was diverted to a new hopper discharge terminal at Stourton. The Balm Road site now houses a maintenance facility for Freightliner Heavy Haul Class 66 locomotives, known as Leeds Midland Road and operated by the London & North Western Railway Company. Unit No 144022 forms the 1234 Leeds to Sheffield service on 19 February 2004. *Both PDS*

STOURTON: The ex-Midland Railway shed at Stourton had just nine months to go before closure when this line-up of Stanier 8F 2-8-0s – Nos 48093, 48311 and 48126 – was recorded on 2 April 1966. Part of the roundhouse shed can be seen on the left. Although Stourton had been on North Eastern Region territory since 1957, it had kept its allocation of predominantly ex-LMS locomotives.

The shed site was cleared soon after closure and part of the land was used for a rail-served steel warehouse. However, steel traffic to Stourton fizzled out in the 1990s and the siding pictured here on 19 February 2004 was thick with rust. *Roger Siviter/PDS*

STOURTON: In this beautifully evocative rendering of the steam age at Stourton, Johnson Midland 2F 0-6-0 waits for a clear signal in one of the down loops. The Midland Railway built extensive sorting sidings here, flanked on the west side by Stourton engine shed, which was to remain active until January 1967.

So often the 'past' photographs of freight activity are matched by 'present' scenes of dereliction or non-railway redevelopment. Not so here! BR chose Stourton as the site of its Freightliner terminal for Leeds, and there has rarely been a quiet moment since its opening in July 1967. Class 66 No 66572 waits on the down through siding on 19 February 2004 with 4E01, the 0214 service from Southampton, while No 66539 awaits its next duty after arriving with 4E58, the 0343 from Ipswich. *David Holmes/PDS*

ROTHWELL: Originally conceived as part of a long-distance route, the grandly titled East & West Yorkshire Union railway never amounted to more than a 5¼-mile link between Stourton on the MR main line and Lofthouse on the GNR approach to Leeds. Passenger services were introduced in 1904 but withdrawn after just nine months because of the competition from trams. The station at Rothwell, however, remained intact and was used by excursion traffic until 1965. A Railway Correspondence & Travel Society special, headed by Ivatt Class 2 2-6-2T No 41273, pauses at Rothwell on 19 May 1962.

Traffic from local collieries declined in the 1960s and the E&WYU closed completely in 1966. Only the terraced houses survived to locate the scene on 27 March 2004. *Gavin Morrison/PDS*

COPLEY HILL: Brand new 'Deltic' Type 5 No D9003 *Meld* undergoes driver training on the 2.5pm Leeds to Doncaster local on 19 September 1961. Meanwhile the old order lives on at Copley Hill shed, with an 'A1' 4-6-2 and a 'J50' 0-6-0 standing outside in the hazy sunshine. The spread of diesels on main-line passenger duties would spell the end for Copley Hill in September 1964.

No features other than the curvature of the line remain in the 'present' picture dated 19 February 2004, as a 'Voyager' unit forms the 1135 Edinburgh to Bristol service. The shed site has long since been redeveloped and the two-track railway is surrounded by ugly high-security fencing. *Gavin Morrison/PDS*

WORTLEY SOUTH JUNCTION: With Copley Hill shed just visible to the right of the signal box, Gresley 'V2' 2-6-2 No 60921 heads south with the 6.21pm Leeds Central to London King's Cross express on 7 July 1959. The track in the foreground is the Wortley curve, which functioned as a 'Leeds avoiding line' for expresses between Wakefield and Bradford after the closure of the Gildersome line in 1965.

Regular use of the Wortley curve ceased in 1984, but a long-running campaign sought to have it retained as a strategic route for Bradford and it was not until 1990 that its closure was formally accepted. A battered sign marks the location of the former junction as a 'Pacer' unit heads into Leeds on 19 February 2004. *Gavin Morrison/PDS*

BEESTON: The LNER started a long tradition of Pullman services on the East Coast Main Line. The 'Queen of Scots' was introduced in the 1920s, running from Glasgow to London King's Cross via Newcastle, Harrogate and Leeds. The name lasted into the British Railways era, and Thompson 'A1' 4-6-2 No 60148 *Aboyeur* passes Beeston Junction with the up service on 5 June 1961. Beeston station had closed to passengers eight years previously.

The 'Queen of Scots' no longer exists, but present-day operator Great North Eastern Railway still runs several named trains aimed at the lucrative business market. On 27 March 2004 the 1605 'White Rose' service from Leeds to King's Cross drifts past the site of Beeston station, formed of a Eurostar unit displaced from its Channel Tunnel duties through lack of patronage. *Gavin Morrison/PDS*

ARDSLEY: The GNR adopted Ardsley as its principal marshalling point for goods traffic in the Leeds and Bradford areas. This early 1960s view, looking north from the road bridge about half a mile south of Ardsley station, shows a typically busy scene with Thompson 'B1' 4-6-0 No 61382 departing from the down sidings, and a 'J50' shunting mineral wagons on the up side.

The opening of Healey Mills yard in 1963 made Ardsley yard redundant and all sidings were eventually removed. The M62 motorway provides a backdrop for the slimmed-down double-track railway, as electric unit No 321902 forms the 1121 stopping service from Leeds to Doncaster on 27 March 2004. *J. F. Ward collection/PDS*

ARDSLEY SHED was opened in 1892 by the GNR, and housed mainly goods engines, although there were some passenger types including 'Pacifics' in later years. BR provided the shed with a new louvre-style roof and a brick screen in 1955, but within a few years its role was to diminish as diesel locomotives ousted steam. This was the scene facing south on 28 February 1960.

Although the shed closed as long ago as 1965, the site had not yet been redeveloped when visited on 27 March 2004. A small forest now covers the area once occupied by sidings on the right. *Noel Machell/ PDS*

A small hint of the labour-intensive nature of steam locomotive servicing is captured on film in May 1954, as 'B1' 4-6-0 No 61377 receives a dose of lubricating oil. *JCH*

HOLBECK DIESEL DEPOT: After the ex-MR shed at Leeds Holbeck closed to steam in 1967, BR converted the former engine repair shop into a diesel depot and built a new diesel servicing shed nearby. Two Class 47s and a Class 08 shunter are visible in this view dated 3 July 1976. The use of train headcodes had recently been discontinued, which explains the '0000' setting displayed on the two Class 47s. Holbeck's allocation of main-line locomotives at that time included members of Classes 31, 45 and 47.

Holbeck lost its main-line locomotive allocation in 1978 but remained open as a diesel servicing point until the early 1990s. The former diesel shed is still in railway-related use as a storage depot for infrastructure materials, as pictured on 21 June 2004. *JCH/PDS*

HOLBECK HIGH LEVEL: An interchange station at Holbeck was opened in 1862, with low-level platforms on the MR/NER line out of Leeds Wellington and high-level platforms on the GNR approach to Leeds Central. Class 'J50' 0-6-0 No 68988 enters Holbeck High Level with a rake of empty coaching stock on 29 April 1949; the first vehicle is No E61606E, an NER-design Corridor Third built at York in 1924.

Both high-level and low-level platforms closed in 1958, and the line to Central was dismantled after all services were diverted to Leeds City in 1967. The former bridge abutment can still be seen on 19 February 2004 as electric unit No 333011 heads out of Leeds on an evening working to Bradford. *H. C. Casserley/PDS*

LEEDS CENTRAL station opened to passengers in July 1848 and survived almost 120 years until closure in May 1967, when a much heralded scheme to concentrate all passenger services on a single Leeds station was achieved. The complexities leading to the opening of Leeds Central were great and it has been stated elsewhere that it 'evolved rather than opened'. Four companies were involved: the GNR, LNWR, Leeds & Thirsk (later NER) and L&YR. In BR days it served the ex-GNR routes to Doncaster and Bradford and the ex-NER route to Harrogate. On 28 February 1960 ex-LNER 'J50' 0-6-0T No 68988 is seen with the empty stock from a King's Cross train.

Today the area is undergoing a transformation with new building and there is nothing left of the station site, as can be seen in the 'present' scene taken on 10 June 2004 from near the River Aire looking north-east towards Wellington Street. *Gavin Morrison/ JCH*

The third picture, also taken on 10 June 2004, shows that a memory of the railway has been left in the shape of a wagon hoist, dating from the 1850s and designed by Sir John Hawkshaw. Its function was to transfer wagons between Wellington Street low-level and high-level goods yards. *JCH*

46

LEEDS CITY: The Midland Railway terminus at Wellington was combined with the ex-LNWR/NER Leeds New station to form Leeds City in 1938. Ex-LMS 2-6-4T No 42093 takes water on 1 June 1963, while a Metropolitan-Cammell DMU waits on the other side of the platform.

Wellington closed to passengers in 1966 but remained in use for many years as a parcels concentration depot. Passenger facilities were reinstated in the 1990s as part of the major rebuilding of Leeds City station. Class 150/2 No 150271 (NL) stands at the new platform 1 with a local train to Knaresborough on 10 March 2004. In the background are some recognisable buildings outside the station. *H. C. Casserley/JCH*

LEEDS CITY: Ex-LNER 'Pacific' 4-6-2 No 60092 *Fairway* enters the station from the York direction on 28 February 1960. The NER had completed this much-needed eastern approach to Leeds in 1869, avoiding the need for east-west trains to reverse.

Following electrification and rationalisation, the approach lines today bear little resemblance to those in the 'past' photograph. Even the buildings on the skyline have changed substantially; perhaps the most definite link between the photographs is the brick wall bordering the railway. On 24 March 2004 a Class 158 arrives from the east with a Middlesbrough to Manchester Airport service, while a Class 150 unit leaves the station. Although the signals have the prefix 'L' for Leeds, they are in fact controlled from York signalling centre. *Gavin Morrison/JCH*

LEEDS CITY: Ex-LNER 'D49' 4-4-0 No 62746 *The Middleton* departs from the west end of Leeds City with a local train to Harrogate on 7 August 1956.

In the second picture ex-LMS 'Jubilee' 4-6-0 No 45675 *Hardy* is at the head of the 8.43pm train to Sheffield on 12 July 1966. By now the major BR reconstruction scheme due for completion in 1967 is well under way, involving a new track layout and passenger facilities as well as the replacement of 17 signal boxes by two men and a computer.

Further rationalisation and the building of new platforms took place in the 1990s and a new £2.2 million interchange with bus stands and taxi rank was opened on 7 March 2004. It is difficult to find any connection between the 'past' photographs and the 'present' view taken on 10 March 2004. Class 158 No 158771 (HT) stands on the right in bay platform 17 with a trans-Pennine service operated by Arriva Trains Northern. *Gavin Morrison/Roger Siviter/JCH*

LEEDS CITY: On 15 August 1981 a six-car DMU enters the station from the west with a Bridlington-bound service, with a Class 110 'Calder Valley' motor composite leading.

Electrification and track remodelling, together with new platforms, have brought many changes. There are now 17 platform faces, with seven through lines, two bays facing east and nine for westbound services. Virgin CrossCountry 'Voyager' No 221122 arrives as the 1058 Bristol Temple Meads to Edinburgh service on 2 March 2004. *Both JCH*

WORTLEY JUNCTION: Not to be confused with Wortley East, West and South Junctions on the GNR approach to Leeds Central, Wortley Junction lay on the NER and MR lines to Harrogate and Keighley respectively. Fairburn Class 4 2-6-4T No 42093 passes the junction with an 11-coach Bristol to Bradford Forster Square working on 9 March 1961. Holbeck Low Level station is visible in the distance, with the GNR line to Leeds Central passing over it at right-angles.

The track layout at Wortley Junction has been drastically simplified, but the north-west exit from Leeds is still busy enough to warrant four tracks. Unit No 333010 forms the 1456 service from Leeds to Skipton on 19 February 2004. *Gavin Morrison/PDS*

FARNLEY JUNCTION was the point where the 13¼-mile 'Leeds New Line', opened in 1900, diverged from the earlier LNWR exit from Leeds via Dewsbury. It ran via Cleckheaton to rejoin the existing route at Spen Valley Junction (Bradley) and enabled LNWR Leeds-Huddersfield trains to avoid the bottleneck formed by the shared use of L&YR tracks between Thornhill and Heaton Lodge Junction. It carried express passenger traffic until 1965, when BR diverted all trains via Dewsbury. English Electric Type 4 (later Class 40) No D257 climbs away from Farnley Junction on the 'New Line' with a trans-Pennine express on 20 July 1962.

Following closure, the trackbed of the 'Leeds New Line' was mostly sold off to adjacent landowners and much of the route is difficult to trace today. At Farnley Junction earthworks for the M621 motorway have swallowed up the embankment that once carried the southbound track, as pictured on 19 February 2004. *Gavin Morrison/PDS*

MORLEY station lies just over 4 miles south of Leeds on the original Huddersfield line. Opened in 1848, it was renamed Morley Low in 1951 to avoid confusion with the GN station at Morley Top; the latter closed in 1961. A Farnley Junction engine, 8F 2-8-0 No 48080, is at the head of the Heaton-Red Bank newspaper empties on 10 June 1966. This train was usually double-headed, hence the use of an 8F.

The station has been modernised, the only facilities now being waiting shelters on each platform. Class 158 No 158808 passes through as the 1137 Leeds-Manchester Piccadilly trans-Pennine service on 2 March 2004, while a Class 142 unit disappears in the distance towards Leeds with a local service from Huddersfield. *Gavin Morrison/JCH*

Dewsbury and Huddersfield

BATLEY: This wonderful view taken in 1960 shows the full extent of the GNR/LNWR joint station at Batley. The two tracks on the right are the LNWR main line from Leeds, curving round towards Dewsbury in the distance. The tracks in the centre and on the left belonged to the GNR, who at one time had four routes radiating from Batley. The line curving sharply to the left was the branch to Runtlings Lane Junction via Chickenley Heath, which had lost its passenger service as early as 1909.

The GNR system around Batley closed in stages, and by the end of 1965 all that remained was a short colliery branch on the former Chickenley Heath line. That branch succumbed in 1972, leaving just the ex-LNWR main line through the station. Unit No 158799 passes through as the 1022 Liverpool Lime Street to Sunderland service on 19 April 2004. *P. Cookson/PDS*

DEWSBURY GNR: Still carrying its LNER number, ex-Great Central 'C14' 4-4-2T No 7444 calls at Dewsbury GNR station with an afternoon train from Wakefield Westgate to Leeds Central on 30 August 1948. The town of Dewsbury was remarkable in having four separate stations, of which two lay on through passenger routes (LNWR and GNR) and two were goods-only termini (L&YR and MR).

After several years of operation with diesel multiple units, British Railways closed the GNR Wakefield-Dewsbury-Batley line to passengers in 1964 and to goods in the following year. The former railway alignment has disappeared under tarmac, as pictured on 19 April 2004. *R. M. Casserley collection/PDS*

LIVERSEDGE: The L&YR Spen Valley line ran from Low Moor to Mirfield, with a branch from Heckmondwike to Thornhill. Both routes lost their passengers status in June 1965 and the Heckmondwike to Mirfield section closed completely at the same, but the line between Low Moor and Thornhill remained open for through freight traffic until 1980. The Railway Correspondence & Travel Society 'South Yorkshire No 5' tour passes through the closed Liversedge station on 23 October 1965, hauled by Mirfield-allocated 8F 2-8-0 No 48202.

A pleasant footpath and cycle track known as the Spen Valley Greenway now threads its way along the trackbed, which was sold to the sustainable transport charity Sustrans in 1999. The 'present' scene is dated 19 April 2004. *Gavin Morrison/PDS*

RAVENSTHORPE station was situated next to Thornhill Junction, where the LNWR line from Leeds joined the L&YR Calder Valley line; the station only ever had platforms on the LNWR tracks. A Calder Valley Class 110 unit, comprising cars E52075, E59707 and E51841, passes through with the 1450 Leeds to Marsden stopping service on 8 July 1983.

Among the more obvious changes in the 'present' view of 19 April 2004 are the absence of Thornhill power station and the reduction from four tracks to two on the ex-L&YR line. Ravensthorpe station is still open for business, but without its LNWR-vintage wooden buildings. Unit No 144006 pulls away with the 1041 Leeds to Huddersfield service on 19 April 2004. *Both PDS*

MIRFIELD: Located on the main line from Huddersfield to Leeds, Mirfield station opened in March 1866, replacing an earlier station dating from 1845. Ex-LMS 4-4-0 No 40552 (20D) heads the 9.05am Manchester Victoria-Normanton train on 21 April 1954. The station was also served by trains from Huddersfield to Bradford Exchange via Cleckheaton.

There is no link with the 'past' photo in today's shot taken on 2 March 2004. There are only basic waiting shelters, the canopies and old buildings having been totally swept away. A Class 142 unit enters the station as the 1134 Huddersfield to Leeds service. Unusually there are two up (westbound) platforms, one on the other face of the island and the second on the far side of the tracks, which is staggered from the island. In the summer of 2004 just one scheduled train (the 1711 from Leeds to Hebden Bridge) used the westbound face of the island, though it is also used on occasion by diverted traffic. *H. C. Casserley/JCH*

MIRFIELD: About three-quarters of a mile west of the station there was once a very busy railway scene, including the eight-road ex-L&YR engine shed. On 16 June 1967, shortly after the closure of the shed, BR 9F 2-10-0 No 92048 passes Mirfield with a westbound rake of four-wheeled oil tanks.

Today the scene is much more pastoral and there are few railway features to link with the 'past' photograph, although there remain one or two recognisable buildings on the skyline. On 6 May 2004 three-car Class 158 unit No 158814 heads west with a trans-Pennine service. *Gavin Morrison/JCH*

HUDDERSFIELD: The first wing of the remarkable station exterior was built in time for the opening of the section of line from Huddersfield to join the L&YR at Heaton Lodge Junction in August 1847. Building was completed by 1850. John Betjeman described it as 'the most splendid station façade in England', with its projecting portico supported by eight Corinthian columns. In the turn-of-the-20th-century photo we see an early motor taxi, various horse-drawn vehicles and a boy (perhaps a pieman?) holding a tray on his head, as he crosses the tram tracks. The trams had been converted from steam to electric traction in 1901-2.

Dominating St George's Square, the building has changed very little in the 150 or so years to today's photo of 12 February 2004. The area in front of the station has been attractively opened out and a young lady checks her mobile phone, perhaps for a text message. The building was threatened with demolition in the 1960s, but the façade and platform 1 were bought by Huddersfield Corporation to mark the centenary of the Borough in 1968, followed by considerable restoration and cleaning of the stonework in 1971. *Courtesy Kirklees Community History Service/JCH*

Below right The statue erected to honour the memory of one of the town's famous sons, Harold Wilson, who served four terms as Prime Minister. *JCH*

HUDDERSFIELD: Ex-LMS 'Jubilee' 4-6-0 No 45632 *Tonga* waits for the 'right away' with the 8.2am Stockport to Leeds City parcels train on 9 October 1963. There appears to be plenty of activity in the goods yard.

On 18 February 2004 Class 150/2 No 150223 awaits departure, forming the 0800 service from Manchester Victoria to Wakefield Westgate, which is hourly between Monday and Saturday. While the ex-LNWR warehouse remains, the goods yard closed in the 1970s and the few sidings that remain are used to stable units between duties. *David Holmes/JCH*

STANDEDGE: Approximately a mile and half west of Marsden station is the entrance to Standedge Tunnel (3 miles 66 yards) beneath the Pennines. When the 'past' photograph was taken on 4 June 1966, there were four tracks through the tunnels, and we see 9F 2-10-0 No 92020 hauling a goods train towards the far left-hand entrance. The first tunnel bore was opened in 1849, the second in 1871 and the third (double line) in 1894.

The two left-hand tunnels closed in October 1966, having been used by the Channel Tunnel Company for ventilation tests before closure. Although the entrances are now partially obscured by trees we have a clear view of EWS Class 60 No 60096 at the head of the 1010 Bredbury-Roxby 'bin liner' train on 27 May 2004. The building on the right is a former canal warehouse and is now the Standedge Visitors Centre, at the start of the longest, highest and deepest canal tunnel in Britain, running from Marsden to Diggle.
Gavin Morrison/JCH

SPRINGWOOD JUNCTION: On 24 May 1959 'Jubilee' 4-6-0 No 45558 *Manitoba* passes Springwood Junction, just west of Huddersfield, where the Penistone branch diverged from the main line to Manchester. The non-corridor coaching stock of this Leeds to Manchester local train would soon be replaced by the first generation of diesel multiple units.

Today's scene is remarkable for the luxuriant tree growth lining the walls of the cutting and filling the space between the two remaining main-line tracks. Unit No 158810 takes the up main line with the 1047 Scarborough to Liverpool Lime Street service on 31 May 2004; the down main line is completely obscured by trees on the left, while the Penistone branch comprises the single track on the right. *Gavin Morrison/PDS*

Around Halifax

HALIFAX: The first station of 1844 was replaced by a second one in 1850, which in turn gave way to the current station in 1855. It was renamed Halifax Old in June 1890 and Halifax Town in 1951, but finally returned to the original title of simply Halifax in 1961! In our turn-of-the-20th-century photo, the separate ticket offices of the L&YR and GNR can clearly be seen.

A new entrance was opened in 1989, seen in the 'present' photograph taken on 25 February 2004. The cobbles remain on the approach road but most of the mills in the distance towards Beacon Hill have disappeared. *J. K. Williams collection/JCH*

HALIFAX: Our photo of 26 March 1977 is dominated by the huge textile mill (Riding Hall Carpets) as a six-car DMU, forming the 1010 Leeds-Manchester Victoria-Southport service, approaches the station. Behind the signal box the trackbed of the former Holmfield line curves away to the left.

Sadly the prosperous manufacturing era has passed and the mills in the background have been demolished. On 10 June 2004 Class 155 unit No 155344 (NL) arrives with the 1449 Leeds-Huddersfield service. *Michael Mensing/JCH*

HALIFAX: Class 5 4-6-0 No 45216, from Bank Hall shed, brings a Leeds to Liverpool express into the station on 24 August 1959. The scene is dominated by textile mills on both sides of the line. The ex-GNR line to Queensbury goes off in the bottom left-hand corner, and the entrance to Beacon Hill Tunnel can be seen in the centre of the picture. The small box is Halifax 'C', which dated back to 1870 as a 'block hut', until superseded by the current signal box (Halifax East).

Today's scene is taken slightly further back and shows the 1884-built signal box from which the 'past' photograph appears to have been taken. It is hard to believe that a branch line once ran round the left-hand side of the box. Many of the mills have gone but recognisable buildings remain on the hillside. On 25 February 2004 Class 144 unit No 144006 (in Metro livery) arrives from the east. *Gavin Morrison/JCH*

HALIFAX: Ex-LMS 4-6-0 'Jubilee' No 45552 *Silver Jubilee* itself stands in the station with a westbound train on 27 May 1960.

Rationalisation of the station layout took place in 1969, reducing the platform faces from five (once six) on three islands to two on a single island. The main building was preserved and is now part of the Eureka! children's museum, having been beautifully restored. As can be seen in the 'present' pictures, taken on 25 February 2004, it now lies outside the station boundary. The third photograph shows the full extent of the original building with Beacon Hill behind.
Gavin Morrison/JCH (2)

HALIFAX: This wonderful view of the town taken from Beacon Hill on 26 August 1959 shows the large goods yard to the left of the church, the end of one of the station platforms on the extreme left above the mill in the bottom left-hand corner, and the Queensbury line passing near the church and sharply curving away to the right of the cooling towers. The main line to Bradford and Leeds can just be seen in the foreground.

Just 45 years later, on 21 August 2004, due to the growth of trees, etc, the same vantage point is not available, but a comparison between the two pictures shows many easily identifiable buildings, including the Halifax Parish Church of St John the Baptist, which is mainly 15th century. A two-car DMU has just left the station and heads towards Beacon Hill Tunnel en route to Bradford. *Gavin Morrison/JCH*

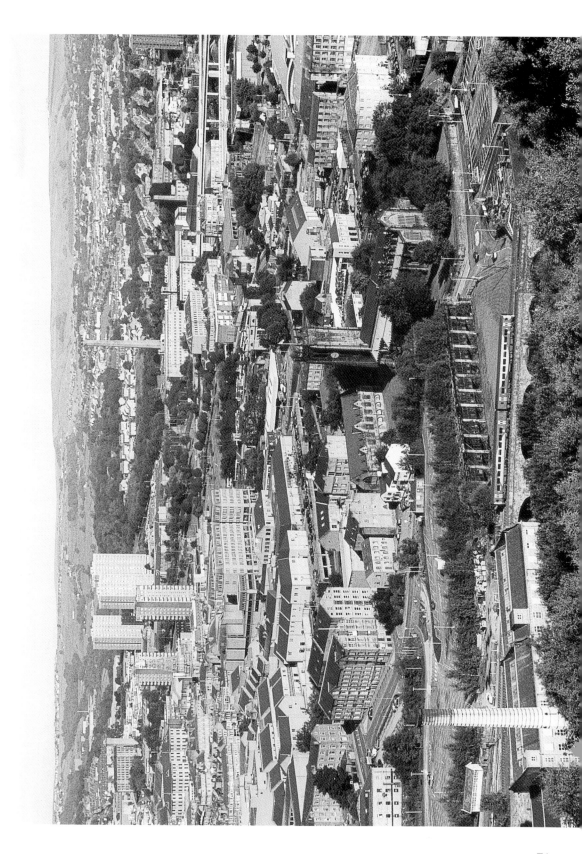

BRIGHOUSE: The first station at Brighouse was opened by the Manchester & Leeds Railway in 1840, but was replaced by a second station 300 yards to the west in 1893. Known as 'Brighouse for Rastrick', it was closed by the British Railways Board in 1970, but re-opened in May 2000, when the station was re-built. In our 'past' picture, taken on 27 September 1959, ex-LMS 4-6-0 'Jubilee' No 45717 *Dauntless* prepares to depart with the 10.30 Liverpool Exchange to Newcastle train.

Comparison with the photograph of 6 May 2004 shows that the main station building has been demolished. An electricity pylon has appeared and modern access ramps have been built for the re-opened station. There is currently an hourly service in each direction between Huddersfield and Leeds via Halifax and Bradford Interchange. *Gavin Morrison/JCH*

SOWERBY BRIDGE station, in the Calder Valley south-west of Halifax, was opened in October 1840 by the Manchester & Leeds Railway and replaced in 1876 by a second station one-third of a mile further east. There was a bay at the east end and ex-LMS 2-6-4T No 42094 simmers quietly with a three-coach local train in October 1959, as the fireman stands on the bunker breaking up any large lumps of coal.

Today the bay no longer remains, although the edge of the platform is clearly to be seen. Behind the trees can just be made out at least one or two of the old mills seen in the 'past' picture. The 'present' photograph is dated **24 March 2004.** *Noel A. Machell/JCH*

MYTHOLMROYD station, between Hebden Bridge and Sowerby Bridge, was opened in May 1847 by the Manchester & Leeds Railway. The photo of 27 April 1961, taken from a westbound train, shows the top of the unusual three-storey building on the down platform, with an upper-quadrant semaphore splitting signal at the far end. Five sets of stairs once led to the booking office and waiting rooms.

In the photo taken on 25 February 2004, although there has been considerable modernisation of the station, the original building still stands but is boarded up; the chimneys have been cut down or removed, and sadly there is the ugly face of graffiti in the foreground. The platforms were rebuilt slightly east of the originals in 1991, with new access ramps replacing the function of the original lift. The remaining old building is Grade 2 listed, but, as it is not maintained, its condition is worsening. The station enjoys a half-hourly service in each direction between Manchester Victoria and either York or Selby. *H. C. Casserley/JCH*

HEBDEN BRIDGE station was opened by the M&L in October 1840. It later became part of the L&YR system and, being Grade 2 listed, retained much of the character of that railway, evading the advance of the corporate image in the 1960s and 1970s. Class 37s Nos 37096 and 37045 head an eastbound oil train on 20 April 1982. At that time loaded oil trains crossed the Pennines in both directions, eastbound from Stanlow to Leeds and westbound from Port Clarence, Haverton Hill and Immingham to various terminals in the North West.

Twenty-two years later, on 17 March 2004, the platform has changed very little but the down loop has been removed. Class 158 unit No 158771 approaches the station with a trans-Pennine service. *Dr L. A. Nixon/JCH*

HALL ROYD JUNCTION is where the Copy Pit line to Burnley leaves the main line from Hebden Bridge to Manchester via Littleborough. On 14 June 1961 2-8-0 'Austerity' No 90181 brings a loaded coal train from Yorkshire and is about to take the Copy Pit line.

There has been some alteration to the tracks, and the signal box and water column have gone, as Class 155 'Super Sprinter' No 155344 (based at Leeds Neville Hill) forms the 1223 service from Manchester Victoria to Selby on 8 April 2003. *Gavin Morrison/JCH*

TODMORDEN station, between Littleborough and Hebden Bridge, was opened by the Manchester & Leeds Railway on 1 January 1841. Looking west from the east end of the station, our undated postcard view shows that the platforms were partly staggered and there was an east-facing bay on the up side. Both main platforms had canopies and the signals were typical L&YR lower-quadrant semaphores.

A much simpler layout is seen in the 'present' picture of 25 February 2004. The down-side (eastbound) platform has a fairly modern waiting shelter but little else, whereas on the opposite platform remain some of the original station buildings. A two-car Class 155 unit (in West Yorkshire Metro livery) approaches from Manchester Victoria with a train for York. The only obvious connection between the pictures is Dobroyd Castle School on the distant hillside, currently run by Buddhists as the Losang Dragpa Centre. *John Ryan collection/JCH*

PELLON was the only intermediate station on the Halifax High Level railway, which ran from Holmfield to St Pauls. The line opened in 1890 and was operated jointly by the GNR and L&YR. It lost its passenger service as early as 1917 but remained open for goods until 1960. In our 'past' picture, taken on 24 May 1959, 2-8-0 'Austerity' No 90122 leaves with the evening freight to Holmfield, apparently a case of 'overkill' from a power point of view!

Sadly the warehouse was demolished following the closure of the line and, apart from the mill chimney in the background, there is nothing to link the two pictures. Today the area has been developed as a modern industrial estate, photographed on Saturday 21 August 2004. *Gavin Morrison/JCH*

LIGHTCLIFFE was one of five intermediate stations between Bradford Exchange and Halifax. Ivatt Class 2 2-6-2T No 41250 arrives at with the Leeds portion of a Bradford to Liverpool express on 5 May 1959.

The station closed in 1965 when BR withdrew stopping trains from the Bradford-Halifax route. The West Yorkshire Passenger Transport Executive proposed building a new Lightcliffe station in the early 1980s, but the plan came to nothing. However, the double-track line pictured on 23 June 2004 is well used by through passenger services, with four trains an hour in each direction on weekdays. *Gavin Morrison/PDS*

The Bradford area

BRADFORD EXCHANGE: Opened in 1850 as Drake Street, the station was re-named Exchange by the L&YR in 1867. In 1973 it was replaced by a new station when the line was shortened by about 185 metres, having been considered too large for current needs, also releasing land for re-development. It was renamed Interchange in 1983, by which time it afforded one of the first purpose-built transport interchanges in the UK between rail and bus. The fine iron trainshed with its two 100-foot spans is shown to good effect as 2-6-4T No 42055 carries out its pilot duties on a bright summer's day in June 1966.

It is difficult today to imagine where Exchange station was situated – the site is now occupied by the Law Courts, as seen in our 'present' picture taken on 24 March 2004. *Dr L. A. Nixon/JCH*

The third photograph records the sad occasion of the last day of steam at the station, Sunday 1 October 1967, with specially cleaned Class 5 4-6-0 No 45428 awaiting departure with the Bradford portion of an express to King's Cross. *Gavin Morrison*

The railways of Bradford.

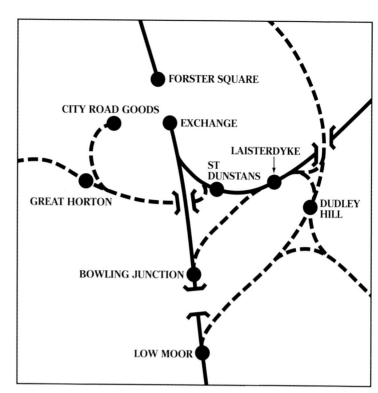

ST DUNSTANS: The GNR extended its Bradford line by just under a mile into the L&YR's terminus in 1867. The connecting line was sharply curved with a 1 in 49 gradient, and St Dunstans station was located on the curve. On 16 April 1957 Fairburn Class 4 2-6-4T No 42235 climbs through the abandoned platforms at St Dunstans – closed five years previously – with the Bradford portion of a King's Cross express.

The 1 in 49 gradient is scarcely an obstacle for today's diesel units. No 158906 climbs out of Bradford with the 1547 service from Blackpool North to Scarborough on 20 April 2004. The air is a lot cleaner than it was in the 1950s! *Gavin Morrison/PDS*

Map labels: FORSTER SQUARE, CITY ROAD GOODS, EXCHANGE, LAISTERDYKE, ST DUNSTANS, GREAT HORTON, DUDLEY HILL, BOWLING JUNCTION, LOW MOOR

LAISTERDYKE was once a busy junction on the GNR approach to Bradford, with routes diverging to Bowling (the 'Bradford avoiding line'), Shipley via Idle, Wakefield via Dudley Hill, and Leeds via the Pudsey loop. Class 'B1' 4-6-0 No 61014 is about to take the Dudley Hill line with coaches for King's Cross on 17 July 1964, while Stanier Class 4 No 42618 stands on the goods lines.

Unit No 158761 passes the much reduced layout at Laisterdyke with the 1547 Blackpool North to Scarborough service on 20 April 2004. The siding on the left gives access to a scrapyard and was still in intermittent use in 2004, with loaded trains running round in Bradford Exchange station before running to Healey Mills yard. *Gavin Morrison/PDS*

DRIGHLINGTON: The GNR line from Bradford to Wakefield via Drighlington lost its local passenger service in 1957 but continued to carry through traffic, including the Bradford portions of King's Cross expresses, until 1966. Drighlington station had already been closed for four years when Fairburn Class 4 2-6-4T was photographed heading towards Wakefield on 30 October 1966. This was the last day of through working over the line.

The Bradford portions of King's Cross expresses were re-routed via the Wortley curve until BR discontinued the practice of splitting and joining trains at Wakefield in 1967. At Drighlington, the A650 road now skirts the former trackbed, as seen on 19 February 2004. *Gavin Morrison/PDS*

BRADFORD SPRINGMILL STREET: A Metropolitan-Cammell three-car unit, Nos E50279, E59108 and E50286, tackles the 1 in 50 climb out of Bradford Exchange with a morning train for Manchester via Halifax on 30 November 1980. On the left is Springmill Street coal depot, which was to survive until 1983 as Bradford's last rail-served coal depot. The GNR Queensbury branch once crossed the waste land on the right before diving under the Halifax line in the foreground.

Two second-generation units pass the same location on 20 April 2004. No 155347 is pulling away with the 1555 Selby to Manchester Victoria service, while in the background No 155343 forms the 1548 Manchester Victoria to Selby. The lines are still controlled from Mill Lane signal box, now set well back from the remaining running lines. *Both PDS*

LOW MOOR: The L&YR shed at Low Moor was opened in 1866 and expanded to 12 roads in 1890. In BR days the shed was partly roofless but was responsible for a sizeable allocation of ex-LMS and ex-LNER locomotives, especially in the years after 1959 when it acquired the engines and men from Hammerton Street shed. Most of the locomotives in this view, facing north on 8 April 1962, are in storage, and include two rebuilt 'Royal Scot' 4-6-0s on the right.

After closure in 1967, the site of Low Moor shed was considered for a possible Freightliner terminal, but the idea was abandoned. Two dogs and their owner enjoy a rest in the nature park that now occupies the site on 20 April 2004. *Industrial Railway Society (J. F. Ward collection)/PDS*

LOW MOOR: A 'Calder Valley' diesel unit, comprising cars E52085, E59696 and E52069, passes the L&YR signal box and former station site at Low Moor as the 0641 Hull to Manchester Victoria service on 29 September 1984. Low Moor had ceased to be a junction by this time, following the closure of the Spen Valley line in 1980, but the box was to remain in use until 1986.

The former railway land on the east side of the line became the base for the West Yorkshire Transport Museum, founded by the West Yorkshire Metropolitan County Council in 1984. The museum planned to demonstrate a range of working trams, trains, trolleybuses and buses at Low Moor and eventually to run trains on the former Spen Valley line. Unfortunately the 'Transperience', as it became known, failed to attract sufficient patronage and its ambitious plans were abandoned. The course of the derelict tramway is visible on the right as unit No 158903 rushes past with the 1650 Leeds to Huddersfield service on 23 June 2004. *Both PDS*

HORTON JUNCTION lay just under 2 miles from Bradford Exchange on the GNR Queensbury branch. LNER 'B7' 4-6-0 No 5052 crosses the junction, having just passed through Horton Park station, with an eastbound excursion in LNER days. The line curving round to the right was the goods-only branch to Bradford City Road.

BR closed the Queensbury branch to passengers in 1955, but the City Road branch and the stub of the Queensbury line as far as Great Horton remained open for goods traffic until 1972. Since then the cutting has been filled in and the site is unrecognisable, as seen on 20 April 2004. *J. F. Ward collection/PDS*

QUEENSBURY was the hub of an unlikely network of lines crossing remote hilly country to connect the mill towns of Bradford, Halifax and Keighley. The station was unusual in being triangular with platforms on all three sides, and the local topography dictated that it was nearly a mile away from the town it claimed to serve. The Railway Correspondence & Travel Society 'West Riding Rail Tour' is pictured in the Bradford to Halifax platform on 6 September 1964, some nine years after the station closed. The DMU used for this tour would have brought disappointment to some, as steam haulage was originally intended.

On 23 June 2004 there are no railway features to identify the site, which is now crossed by a public footpath.
T. J. Edgington/PDS

THORNTON: The 'West Riding Rail Tour' of 6 September 1964 is pictured again at Thornton, which by now was the end of a branch from Bradford via Queensbury. The line had closed as a through route to Keighley in 1956, one year after the withdrawal of passenger services. After a suitable pause for photography, the tour would retrace its steps to Bradford and follow a circuitous route around the railway byways of the West Riding, visiting Dudley Hill, Batley (GNR and LNWR), Kirkburton, Meltham, Holmfirth, Clayton West, Barnsley, Healey Mills and Shipley via Idle – quite an impressive itinerary!

Goods traffic to Thornton ceased in 1965 and much of the trackbed was sold off to local landowners. The station site is now occupied by Thornton Primary School, whose playing fields are pictured on 23 June 2004. *T. J. Edgington/PDS*

DENHOLME station was beyond Thornton on the GNR line from Queensbury to Keighley, and opened in January 1884. Out in open country, the station was 850 feet above sea level, close to Doe Park Reservoir, as seen in this postcard view, probably taken around the turn of the 20th century. The station consisted of an island platform together with signal box and station buildings. It appears that the goods yard contained wagons of coal being unloaded into two horse-drawn wagons, no doubt destined for one of the woollen mills in the district.

Denholme closed to passengers in 1955 and to goods in 1961, and today there is nothing left of the railway other than a 'Station Road' sign. A large timber yard occupies the station area as can be seen in our 'present' photograph taken on 21 August 2004. The reservoir and the hillside behind provide enduring links with the 'past' picture. *John Ryan collection/JCH*

BRADFORD FORSTER SQUARE had its origins as Bradford Market Street, opened by the Leeds & Bradford Railway in 1846. That station was replaced by Bradford Midland, on an adjacent site, in March 1890, renamed Forster Square by the LMS in 1924. With much disused track in evidence, a two-car Derby Class 108 DMU formed of E54195 and E53620 passes the signal box as it arrives with the 0930 service from Ilkley on 29 September 1984.

The loss of the once heavy parcels traffic from Bradford and the prospect of releasing valuable land for redevelopment led BR to relocate Forster Square station in 1990 to a more compact site 120 yards to the north-west, and by the end of 1994 overhead electrification was complete. The new station has only three platforms with no loco-release facilities and nearly all the services are operated by Class 333 EMUs (having replaced the 308s) to Skipton, Ilkley or Leeds, as seen on 6 May 2004 with a Class 333 awaiting departure to Skipton. However, GNER Class 91-hauled trains continue to run between Bradford Forster Square and London King's Cross, including 'The Yorkshire Pullman' on weekdays. *PDS/JCH*

Inside Forster Square on 11 June 1947, ex-Midland 4-4-0 No 484 (allocated to 20F Skipton) heads the 5.03pm train to Leeds. *H. C. Casserley*

BRADFORD VALLEY GOODS: Looking north-west from the station, on 13 September 1976, Bradford Valley goods depot provides the backdrop for Class 31s Nos 31319 and 31312 awaiting their next duties. The industrial landscape is still intact, including a power station – the square buildings were early cooling towers made of wood, while a more modern one can be seen to the rear.

On 10 June 2004 the scene is unrecognisable. Valley freight terminal closed in August 1984, its traffic being diverted to Leeds Whitehall until that too closed in 1990. In the background the heavy industry has disappeared and the former goods yard has been colonised by the retail trade. A Class 333 unit arrives with a service from Ilkley. *Michael Mensing/JCH*

MANNINGHAM: Class 'D49/2' 4-4-0 No 62736 *The Bramham Moor* leaves Manningham station with an evening train for Harrogate via Otley on 3 July 1956. The use of ex-LNER locomotives on this former Midland Railway line had its origins in the late 19th century, when the NER obtained running powers to run trains from Harrogate into the MR terminus.

Manningham station closed to passengers together with neighbouring Frizinghall in 1965. Although Frizinghall regained a station in 1987, Manningham has never been considered a high priority for re-opening. The 'present' photograph is dated 20 April 2004. *Gavin Morrison/PDS*

MANNINGHAM: The Midland Railway opened Manningham shed in 1872. It retained its Midland flavour into BR days, but its allocation in the 1950s included some ex-L&YR '2P' Radial tank engines, including Nos 50795 and 50636, which are pictured in store outside the shed on 18 May 1957.

After a long period of decline, the shed closed in 1967. The site is now occupied by an industrial estate, pictured on 20 April 2004. The appearance of a new hill on the skyline is disconcerting – it is in fact a spoil tip produced by local quarrying. *Gavin Morrison/PDS*

Airedale and Wharfedale

KIRKSTALL: 'Deltic' No D9005 *The Prince of Wales's Own Regiment of Yorkshire* passes the closed station of Kirkstall with the 'Hadrian Flyer' on 17 June 1967. This train covered the 86.8 miles from Carlisle to Skipton in 72 minutes 47 seconds, which is believed to have been a record. Two of the four tracks along the Aire Valley had just been taken out of use following the withdrawal of the Leeds-Shipley-Bradford local service.

Passengers on the comparatively long-distance service between Leeds and Morecambe often travel in older and less comfortable trains than those that ply between Leeds, Bradford and Ilkley. 'Pacer' unit No 142094 forms the 1258 Morecambe to Leeds service on 26 March 2004. *Gavin Morrison/PDS*

NEWLAY & HORSFORTH: The Midland main line between Leeds and Keighley carried a varied mixture of express passenger, local passenger and goods traffic. Fairburn Class 4 2-6-4T No 42139 passes Newlay with a Bristol to Bradford Forster Square express on 11 May 1961. Local services were mainly in the hands of DMUs by this time.

All intermediate stations between Leeds and Shipley closed in 1965, and the case for re-opening them is poor because the railway runs along the valley bottom and avoids the most densely populated areas. Unit No 333001 passes the former station site with the 1411 Ilkley to Leeds service on 26 March 2004. *Gavin Morrison/PDS*

RODLEY & CALVERLEY: A Metropolitan-Cammell two-car unit, headed by car E51286, pulls away from Rodley & Calverley with a local service to Leeds on 16 April 1961. One of the up sidings is being used to stable spare coaching stock for the summer season, while the goods yard on the left would still have been in daily use at that time.

The daytime electric service from Shipley to Leeds comprises four trains an hour at the time of writing, together with two trains from Ilkley, which join the main line at Apperley Junction – a far more frequent service than was provided in quadruple-track days. Unit No 333003 forms the 1402 Bradford Forster Square to Leeds service on 26 March 2004. *Gavin Morrison/PDS*

SHIPLEY: A few hundred yards to the south of the station, on the west side of the Bradford Forster Square line, 4MT 2-6-0 No 43039 passes Shipley goods yard with a Leeds to Bradford service on 15 August 1959. The yard contains a variety of open trucks and closed vans. Note the array of signals in the distance, for trains entering the triangular junction station.

In the second photo, taken on 16 July 1990, the goods yard is occupied by Crossley & Evans, still producing rail traffic in the form of a daily trainload of scrap metal. Class 37 No 37054 waits while a consist of POA wagons is prepared by the firm's resident Hunslet shunter.

On 10 June 2004 the third shot confirms that the yard remains very active, although now served once a week instead of every day. A line of loaded wagons stand by the main line waiting collection. By now the line has been electrified and a Class 333 heads towards Shipley from Bradford.
Gavin Morrison/PDS/JCH

SHIPLEY station is almost unique on Network Rail, sharing with Earlestown the distinction of having platforms on each side of a triangle. The first station for Shipley was opened in 1846 by the Leeds & Bradford Railway, but was replaced in 1875 by the existing station a couple of hundred yards to the north. On 29 August 1986 Class 31 No 31282 takes the Bradford to Leeds curve with 8K58, the 1250 Shipley-Hunslet scrap train. Shipley Bradford Junction signal box, built by the Midland Railway in 1903, is beyond the semaphore signal. To the right of the locomotive can be seen the western side of the triangle, which is the Bradford to Keighley line.

The distinctive station canopy has gone, as have the signal box and semaphores, electrification having taken place in 1985. A Class 333 unit arrives at the station with a Bradford to Leeds service on 10 March 2004, at which time attractive new platform waiting rooms were being built on both platforms of the Leeds-Bradford side of the triangle. *PDS/JCH*

SHIPLEY: During the summer of 1956 the English Electric Co-Co 'Deltic' prototype is seen on the Bradford-Skipton side of the triangle. Although the prototype was only to have a short working life – it failed at Doncaster in 1961 and was never returned to service – it paved the way for BR's production fleet of 22 'Deltics' and its significance in railway history was recognised through its preservation at the Science Museum in London.

Although there is now no canopy, quite a lot of the station building remains, as seen on 10 March 2004, with unit No 333007 forming a Bradford Forster Square-Skipton service. Only one platform face is in use on this south-west side of the station, due to limited clearances on the sharp curve. *Gavin Morrison/JCH*

SHIPLEY: Type 4 D276 (later to become Class 40 No 40076) takes the west-east curve on 20 April 1961. The engine was allocated to York shed from new, and is being employed here on crew training.

In the 'present' photo, taken on 24 March 2004, Class 333 No 333002 departs with a Leeds-Skipton service. Changes include the overhead wires of electrification, the addition of platforms on this side of the triangle and the removal of the crossover, but the buildings in the background remain much the same. *Gavin Morrison/JCH*

CROSSFLATTS, between Shipley and Keighley, did not have a station until May 1982. On Saturday 8 November 1958 an unidentified 'Black Five' 4-6-0 is piloted by ex-Midland 4-4-0 No 40491 on the down 'Waverley' from London St Pancras to Edinburgh.

On 6 May 2004 'Pacer' No 144001 forms the 1258 service from Morecambe to Leeds. The major differences include the reduction in tracks from four to two, the wires and supports of electrification, and of course a station where there was not one before. The buildings on the left link the two pictures, but what cannot be seen below the bank on the left, parallel to the railway, is the relatively new A629 Aire Valley relief road, which carries a great deal of traffic. *Gavin Morrison/JCH*

KEIGHLEY (MAIN LINE): Situated approximately halfway between Shipley and Skipton, the first station was opened by the Leeds & Bradford Extension in 1847. It was replaced by the present station in 1883, by the Midland Railway. A junction station for the branch line to Oxenhope, it is today one of the few Network Rail stations to be shared with a preservation society. Platforms 1 and 2 serve the main line and 3 and 4 serve the branch. In our 'past' photograph dated 24 June 1905, looking north-west towards Skipton, we see tidy platforms with a number of passengers waiting for a Bradford or Leeds train.

On 13 April 2004, disappearing away on the left is the rear car of 'Super Sprinter' No 156469 forming the 0947 Leeds to Carlisle service. On the right is Class 333 No 333009 with a Skipton to Bradford Forster Square working. While the station canopies have mostly gone, as has the bay on the right, the building beyond remains. *R. M. Casserley collection/JCH*

KEIGHLEY (BRANCH PLATFORMS): The Worth Valley branch opened in 1867, originally with stations at Ingrow, Haworth and Oxenhope. It was closed by the British Transport Commission in 1962, but rescued for preservation and re-opened in 1968. On 17 October 1946 ex-GNR 'N1' 0-6-2T No 9449 stands with the 12.10pm train from Bradford Exchange, having joined the Oxenhope branch just outside Keighley station.

On 13 April 2004 Ivatt 2-6-2T No 41241, looking superb, arrives with the 1115 train from Oxenhope, operated by the K&WVR. While the canopies on the near platform have gone, most remain on the opposite side. The signal box on the left near the platform end is a comparatively recent addition to the railway, having been moved from Shipley Bingley Junction after the resignalling of Shipley in 1994. No 41241 will run round its train before heading back to Oxenhope as the 1200 departure. *H. C. Casserley/JCH*

OAKWORTH was just an insignificant branch-line station when this 1950s scene was recorded with Ivatt 2-6-2T No 41273 heading a Keighley-Oxenhope train. It would be a push-and-pull working, the engine being allocated to the sub-shed at Keighley for use on the branch.

The station was closed in 1962, but more than half a century after the 'past' photograph, on 13 April 2004, the station is immaculate, having been fully restored by the Keighley & Worth Valley Railway. One of the resident railbuses, No 79964, calls with a Keighley-Oxenhope service. *Gavin Morrison/JCH*

OXENHOPE was the terminus of the 4¾-mile branch from Keighley, opened in 1867 by the Midland Railway. Looking towards Haworth, ex-MR Johnson 0-4-4T No 1275, at the head of a two-coach push-and-pull train, has just arrived with the 1.15pm service from Keighley on 17 October 1946. The LMS timetable of October 1947 shows nine trains in each direction on Mondays to Fridays, and 12 on Saturdays. The station appears deserted and it is perhaps no surprise that the branch closed in 1962, just before publication of the first Beeching Report.

On 13 April 2004 the 1200 train from Keighley has been brought in by Ivatt 2-6-2T No 41241. The platform is crowded because it is the Tuesday after Easter, which is still a holiday in parts of West Yorkshire. *H. C. Casserley/JCH*

YEADON: The 1¼-mile branch to Yeadon was conceived as part of a through route between Guiseley on the Leeds-Ilkley line and Horsforth on the Leeds-Harrogate line. Only the section between Guiseley and Yeadon was built and – despite the platform in this photograph – it never supported a regular passenger service. Class 'N1' 0-6-2T No 69430 brings a rare burst of activity to Yeadon with a Stephenson Locomotive Society/Manchester Locomotive Society special on 6 September 1953.

The Yeadon branch closed in 1964 and a highways maintenance depot has since been established on the site. The 'present' picture is dated 20 April 2004. *T. J. Edgington/PDS*

GUISELEY station retained many period features when photographed on 29 November 1980, with a Metropolitan-Cammell two-car unit forming a Leeds to Ilkley service. Behind the lattice footbridge is the Midland Railway signal box, erected in 1909, and behind the box is the station goods yard, which was still receiving wagonloads of coal in the late 1970s.

The signal box gained a panel for new colour-light signalling in 1983 but closed in 1994 when the line was comprehensively resignalled in readiness for electrification. Unit No 333013 forms the 1322 Ilkley to Bradford Forster Square service on 20 April 2004. *Both PDS*

MENSTON: Ex-NER Class 'D20' 4-4-0 No 2393 approaches Menston with the 5.15pm Bradford to Harrogate service on 11 June 1947. It will take the Otley line shortly after leaving Menston and will join the Leeds-Harrogate line at Arthington.

The all-year-round Bradford to Harrogate service ceased in 1957, but Menston continued to be served by trains from Leeds and Bradford to Ilkley. These too were threatened with withdrawal in 1968, but after many years of uncertainty the branch was electrified in 1995 and now enjoys an efficient and well-used commuter service. Unit No 333010 departs as the 1311 Ilkley to Leeds service on 20 April 2004. *H. C. Casserley/PDS*

ARTHINGTON: The Otley line formed a triangle where it met the Leeds-Harrogate line at Arthington, but platforms were provided only on the Leeds-Harrogate and Leeds-Otley faces. The station is pictured from the Leeds end on 25 April 1954.

The location of Arthington station owed more to railway geography than to local people's needs – the small village of Arthington was about a mile away – yet it remained open until the Otley line closed in 1965. A visit on 26 March 2004 found the former station area privately occupied, flanked by the still active Leeds-Harrogate line. *H. C. Casserley/PDS*

OTLEY: The line from Arthington to Otley was built by the NER but its continuation from Otley to Menston and Burley was a joint venture between the NER and the MR. The same pattern continued after the 1923 Grouping, with the Otley-Menston/Burley line operated jointly by the LNER and the LMS. On 11 June 1947 LNER Class 'G5' 0-4-4T No 7240 approaches Otley station with the 5.28pm Leeds City to Ilkley train. The first coach is an ex-GCR railmotor.

Otley station survived just long enough to achieve its centenary in 1965. After that, the line was soon dismantled, and in the 1980s the Otley bypass road was constructed alongside the trackbed. The 'present' photograph is dated 20 April 2004. *H. C. Casserley/PDS*

ILKLEY station was opened by the MR and NER (Otley & Ilkley Joint Railway) on 1 August 1865. Undoubtedly the railway shared in the prosperity of the town, which became a spa after the discovery of sulphur that was suitable for curing some skin diseases. It later became a through station with the completion of the line to Skipton via Bolton Abbey; however, that section was closed in 1965. A two-car Metropolitan-Cammell DMU, comprising cars E50257 and E56090, has just left the station with the 1705 service to Leeds on 21 July 1982.

The attractive hipped-roof signal box closed in 1994, shortly before electrification; colour light signals had already replaced the semaphores in 1983. On 10 March 2004 Class 333 unit No 333008 is arriving from Bradford Forster Square; it is passing the site of the demolished signal box, but the two buildings close by remain. The tower on the skyline can just be seen in the 'present' picture just to the right of the second building. *PDS/JCH*

On the trackbed of the former through lines to Skipton the canopies are in place but the area is now a car park with a supermarket at the far end. *JCH*

BOLTON ABBEY: Located between Ilkley and Skipton, the station dates back to 1888, when the Midland Railway completed the line to Skipton. It was closed by British Railways in 1965 but subsequently re-opened as part of the Embsay & Bolton Abbey Steam Railway. The view is looking towards Skipton on 25 April 1954.

Today the down platform has been removed together with its buildings, so all services use the former up platform where the station buildings remain as seen in the 'present' picture of 15 August 2000. *H. C. Casserley/JCH*

KILDWICK & CROSSHILLS: The first station here was opened by the Leeds & Bradford Railway in 1848 as 'Kildwick', re-named 'Kildwick & Cross Hills' in 1863, before reaching the final title of 'Kildwick & Crosshills' after 1 January 1884. It closed in 1889 to be replaced by a new station a few hundred yards to the east, which lasted until final closure by British Railways in 1965. On 18 April 1967 Class 9F 2-10-0 No 92223 heads a southbound mixed goods train through the closed station.

The line was electrified in 1995, but apart from the wall on the right nothing can be seen of the former station. A Class 333 EMU passes through as a Skipton to Leeds service on 13 April 2004. *Gavin Morrison/JCH*

Skipton and the Dales

SKIPTON: With only just over two years to the end of steam, BR Standard 4MT 4-6-0 No 75019 drifts through the station on 8 August 1966 with a trainload of empty unfitted mineral wagons, believed to be from Colne to Stourton. A Cravens DMU (later Class 105) can be seen on the left and a Metropolitan-Cammell type (later Class 101) in the bay on the right.

Nearly 40 years have gone by, but apart from electrification, new lights and removal of semaphore signals there has been little apparent change between the two photographs, the 'present' one taken on 17 March 2004. Class 333 unit No 333006 with MetroTrain branding has just arrived from Leeds. These units were manufactured by Siemens in 2001; they were delivered as three-car sets, but later augmented to four cars. *Noel A. Machell/JCH*

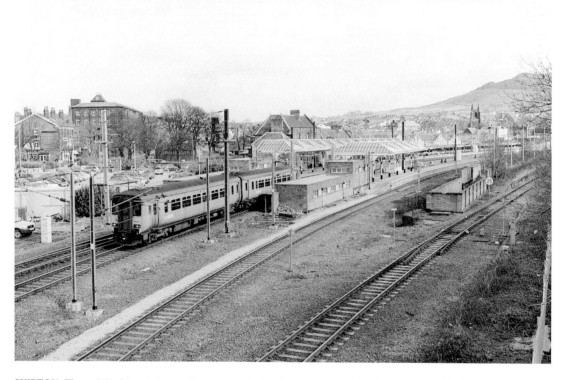

SKIPTON: The original Leeds & Bradford Extension Railway station of 1847 was replaced in 1876 by a new one 200 yards to the south. Often referred to as the 'gateway to the S&C', even today the station retains a great deal of its Midland Railway character. In our 'past' picture of 28 April 1949, ex-L&YR 2-4-2T No 10622 leaves the station with a two-coach westbound service, probably a local to Colne. Note the height of the signal post, which would be to ensure visibility over a road bridge.

By the time the second photo was taken, on 6 June 1987, a number of changes had taken place. The cattle dock in the goods yard on the left is overgrown and out of use, the entrances to the subway have been replaced by modern structures, and the tall semaphore has been substituted by a much shorter upper-quadrant. It appears that the glass canopy station roof has been restored. 'Celebrity' green-liveried Class 40 No D200 (40122) heads north-west with the 1625 Leeds to Carlisle service.

The principal changes seen in the third picture of 17 March 2004 are the simplification of the tracks, the conversion of the goods yard into a car park and the completion of electrification from Leeds and Bradford in 1995. The mill in the background has lost its chimney, while the station buildings and canopies are much the same. Class 156 'Super Sprinter' No 156444 forms the 1249 Leeds to Carlisle service. *H. C. Casserley/PDS/JCH*

GRASSINGTON & THRESHFIELD opened in 1902 as 'Grassington', but in the same year had 'Threshfield' added. It closed to regular services in 1930 but continued to be used by excursions on Bank Holidays and the occasional steam special until 1966, by which time it was known simply as Grassington. Goods traffic survived until 1969. On 10 April 1950 ex-Midland 0-6-0 No 44041 heads the empty stock of a ramblers' excursion.

Most of the branch remains open to carry limestone from Rylstone quarry, but absolutely nothing remains of the former branch terminus apart from a shallow cutting on the approach to the station. Nevertheless, the village stores on Station Road provides a definite link between the 'past' and 'present' photographs, the latter taken on 12 May 2004. *T. J. Edgington/JCH*

EARBY: The Leeds & Bradford Railway (later part of the Midland Railway) extended its tracks from Skipton to Colne as early as 1848. This stretch, together with the short branch from Earby to Barnoldswick, remained open into BR days, although it carried mainly local traffic and did not live up to its potential as a through trans-Pennine route. Stanier 4MT 2-6-4T No 42549 calls at Earby with the 4.30pm train from Skipton to Barnoldswick on 19 March 1955.

The Barnoldswick branch closed to passengers in 1965 and to goods in the following year, while the Skipton to Colne line survived until 1970. A vigorous campaign has been mounted in recent years to re-instate the Skipton-Colne link, but for the time being the former trackbed at Earby makes a pleasant footpath, as seen on 23 January 2003. *T. J. Edgington/PDS*

GARGRAVE is the first station out of Skipton towards Hellifield, opened by the 'Little' North Western in 1849. That company was incorporated in 1846 to connect Skipton with Lancaster and Low Gill on the Lancaster & Carlisle Railway, which was then under construction. The unofficial 'Little' was to distinguish this enterprise from the London & North Western Railway, which had been incorporated about the same time. The 'Little' North Western later became part of the Midland Railway. On 11 May 1966 BR Standard 4MT No 75058 heads north through Gargrave with tank wagons.

Nearly 40 years later, on 12 May 2004, the scene has changed very little. The station remains well maintained, despite having lost its staff in 1970. The 0819 service from Leeds to Morecambe is formed of Class 144 No 144011. *Roger Siviter/JCH*

HELLIFIELD: This old postcard, perhaps from around the turn of the 20th century, shows the up side of the main island platform looking north, with the engine shed in the distance on the right-hand side. Three very smart station staff pose for the photographer. It is recorded that in 1903 some 80 men worked at the shed and there were 22 sets of drivers/firemen working passenger and freight turns. Even by nationalisation the shed still had an allocation of 33 engines.

Although the scene on 12 May 2004 is instantly recognisable, the shed and nearly all the sidings have gone and the station is a shadow of its former self. Back in April 1948 more than 70 trains used the station each day, whereas in the summer of 2004 the total stood at less than 20. *John Ryan collection/JCH*

HELLIFIELD: At the south end of the station, again looking north, LMS 2-6-2T No 21 (BR No 40021) stands in the bay waiting to be coupled to a four-coach train on 28 April 1949.

In the 'present' picture of 12 May 2004 the fence on the left indicates where the bay was situated. *H. C. Casserley/JCH*

HELLIFIELD: On 21 December 1963 'Jubilee' 4-6-0 No 45629 *Straits Settlements* stands in the north-end bay with the 12 noon train to Carlisle.

More than 40 years later, on 12 May 2004, we see a sharp contrast between the weed-infested platform flanking the closed bay and the meticulously refurbished canopies of the station. Class 156 unit No 156428 forms a Leeds-Carlisle service. *Gavin Morrison/JCH*

LONG PRESTON is situated between Hellifield and Settle Junction. This 1964 scene, looking north, shows ex-LMS 0-6-0 No 44197 propelling an engineers' train past the signal box towards Settle Junction. The photographer recalls that the train was travelling at speed and continued some distance beyond the station, possibly operating under special ballast train conditions.

On 12 May 2004, looking from the nearby road overbridge, the siding on the left has gone and only basic up and down tracks remain. The signal box closed in 1971 and the station has been since modernised. A Freightliner Heavy Haul Class 66 heads north with empty coal hoppers returning to Scotland via the S&C. *David Holmes/JCH*

CLAPHAM station opened on 1 August 1849 on the line from Settle Junction to Carnforth, and until 1954 it was the junction for the branch to Low Gill on the West Coast Main Line. On 13 June 1947 ex-LMS 2-6-2T No 16 enters the station with the 3.18pm train from Low Gill; the main line to Carnforth curves away to the left. According to the timetable for 1947 there were only two trains each day on the branch between Clapham and Low Gill, although there were additional services between Clapham and Ingleton.

More than 50 years have elapsed between the two photographs. On 12 May 2004 nothing remains of the yard or the line to Low Gill, although the house on the right provides an excellent link. The signal box closed in 1968. 'Pacer' unit No 144011 (based at Neville Hill depot, Leeds) comes round the curve, preparing to stop with the 1024 service from Morecambe to Leeds. *H. C. Casserley/JCH*

HORTON IN RIBBLESDALE was opened by the Midland Railway in May 1876 as 'Horton', subsequently renamed 'Horton-in-Ribblesdale' (with hyphens) in 1927 by the LMS. The Midland Railway signal box was still in use when Class 40 No 40124 was photographed on 23 June 1982 heading 6S52, the 0505 Winsford-Mossend rock salt train.

The box closed in May 1984 and all sidings and points were removed. On 12 May 2004 Class 156 'Super Sprinter' No 156471 leads a four-car formation on the 1029 service from Leeds to Carlisle. The station is beautifully maintained, despite the absence of railway staff. The line is well used by freight traffic including coal from Scotland to power stations in the Aire and Trent valleys and containerised gypsum from Drax to Newbiggin. *PDS/JCH*